UNDERSTANDING
HUMANS

Foreword by
David Edmonds

UNDERSTANDING
HUMANS

HOW SOCIAL
SCIENCE
CAN HELP
SOLVE OUR
PROBLEMS

S Sage

1 Oliver's Yard
55 City Road
London EC1Y 1SP

2455 Teller Road
Thousand Oaks
California 91320

Unit No 323-333, Third Floor, F-Block
International Trade Tower
Nehru Place, New Delhi – 110 019

8 Marina View Suite 43-053
Asia Square Tower 1
Singapore 018960

Editor: Natalie Aguilera
Editorial assistant: Sarah Moorhouse
Production editor: Ian Antcliff
Marketing manager: Fauzia Eastwood
Cover design: Shaun Mercier
Typeset by: C&M Digitals (P) Ltd, Chennai, India
Printed in the UK

Library of Congress Control Number: 2023938605

British Library Cataloguing in Publication data

A catalogue record for this book is available
from the British Library

ISBN 978-1-5296-8017-1 (pbk)

CONTENTS

ABOUT THE
CONTRIBUTORS

Mahzarin Banaji is Richard Clarke Cabot Professor of Social Ethics at Harvard University. She studies thinking and feeling as they unfold in social context, with a focus on mental systems that operate in implicit or unconscious modes. She also serves as the first Carol K. Pforzheimer Professor at the Radcliffe Institute for Advanced Study, and as the George A. and Helen Dunham Cowan Chair in Human Dynamics at the Santa Fe Institute.

Gurminder K. Bhambra is Professor of Postcolonial and Decolonial Studies in the Department of International Relations in the School of Global Studies, University of Sussex. She is a Fellow of the British Academy, of the Academy of Social Sciences, and the Royal Historical Society. She is President of the British Sociological Association (2022–24) and is currently working on her Leverhulme Trust Major Research Fellowship project (2022–24), 'Varieties of Colonialism, Varieties of Empire'.

Jo Boaler is a Professor at the Stanford Graduate School of Education. Her research focuses on mathematics teaching and learning, in particular, how different teaching approaches impact students' learning, how to teach mathematics for a 'growth mindset', and how equity is promoted in mathematics classrooms. She is also a Member of the Wu Tsai Neurosciences Institute.

Janet Carsten is Professor Emerita of Social and Cultural Anthropology at the University of Edinburgh who has researched widely in Malaysia and Britain. She is the author of eight books and specialises in kinship and relatedness.

Erica Chenoweth is the Frank Stanton Professor of the First Amendment at Harvard Kennedy School and a Susan S. and Kenneth L. Wallach Professor at the Radcliffe Institute for Advanced Studies at Harvard University. They study political violence and its alternatives. At Harvard,

Chenoweth directs the Nonviolent Action Lab, an innovation hub that provides empirical evidence in support of movement-led political transformation.

Valerie Curtis (1958–2020) was a British scientist who was Director of the Environmental Health Group at the London School of Hygiene and Tropical Medicine. Curtis had a background in engineering, epidemiology and anthropology, and had a particular interest in human behaviour around hygiene, especially from an evolutionary perspective. Curtis was an advisor to governments including, in India and Tanzania, on sanitation campaigns. She advised the UK government during the 2020 coronavirus pandemic, as a member of the Scientific Pandemic Influenza Group on Behaviours (SPI-B), on how to encourage people to adhere to recommendations.

Sam Friedman is a Professor of Sociology at London School of Economics. He is a sociologist of class and inequality whose research focuses in particular on the cultural dimensions of contemporary class division. He is currently writing a book with Aaron Reeves (under contract with Harvard University Press) exploring how the British elite has changed over the last 120 years.

Jonathan Haidt is Thomas Cooley Professor of Ethical Leadership at New York University Stern School of Business. Haidt's research examines the intuitive foundations of morality, and how morality varies across cultures – including the cultures of progressives, conservatives, and libertarians. Haidt is the author of The New York Times' bestsellers *The Righteous Mind: Why Good People are Divided by Politics and Religion* (2012), and *The Coddling of the American Mind: How Good Intentions Are Setting Up a Generation for Failure* (2018).

David Halpern is President and Founding Director of the Behavioural Insights Team. David was previously the first Research Director of the Institute for Government and between 2001 and 2007 was the Chief Analyst at the Prime Minister's Strategy Unit. David was also appointed as the What Works National Advisor in July 2013, leading efforts to improve the use of evidence across the UK government. Before entering govern-ment, David held posts at Cambridge, Oxford and Harvard universities. He has written several books and papers on areas relating to behavioural insights and well-being, including *The Hidden Wealth of Nations* (2010) and *Online Harms and Manipulation* (2019).

Bruce Hood is Professor of Developmental Psychology in Society in the School of Psychological Science at the University of Bristol. His research interests include the science of happiness and cognitive development from a neuroscience perspective. He is the author of numerous journal articles and book chapters and frequently conducts research projects at Bristol.

Daniel Kahneman is an Israeli-American psychologist and economist notable for his work on the psychology of judgement and decision-making, as well as behavioural economics, for which he was awarded the 2002 Nobel Memorial Prize in Economic Sciences. He is Professor Emeritus of Psychology and Public Affairs at Princeton University's Princeton School of Public and International Affairs. Kahneman is a founding partner of TGG Group, a business and philanthropy consulting company.

Alison Liebling is Professor of Criminology and Criminal Justice at the University of Cambridge and the Director of the Institute of Criminology's Prisons Research Centre. She has extensive expertise in prisons, having carried out research on wide-ranging topics including suicide and self-harm, close supervision centres for difficult prisoners, and conceptualising and measuring the moral quality of prison life. The 'moral climate' survey she developed with Helen Arnold and others has been used or adapted internationally in many penal systems.

Stephen Reicher is Professor of Psychology and Neuroscience at the University of St. Andrews. His research focuses on the issues of group behaviour and the individual–social relationship. He is currently starting work on a Leverhulme funded project looking at the impact of devolution on Scottish identity and social action in Scotland.

Jennifer Richeson is Philip R. Allen Professor of Psychology at Yale University. Her research examines multiple psychological phenomena related to cultural diversity. Much of Richeson's recent research considers how people reason about and respond to societal inequality and injustice. Richeson has written book chapters on a wide range of subjects, from ageism to intergroup interactions and stereotyping.

Saskia Sassen is the Robert S. Lynd Professor of Sociology and co-chairs the Committee on Global Thought at Columbia University. Her recent books are *Territory, Authority, Rights: From Medieval to Global Assemblages* (2008), *A Sociology of Globalization* (2007), and the 4th fully updated edition of *Cities in a World Economy* (2011). Her books have been translated into 21 languages.

Hetan Shah is Chief Executive at the British Academy, the UK's national academy for humanities and social sciences. He is Chair of Our World in Data, which brings together research and data to make progress against the world's largest problems. He is Visiting Professor at the Policy Institute, Kings College London and a Fellow at Birkbeck, University of London. Hetan serves on several advisory boards including the Bennett Institute for Public Policy at the University of Cambridge, the UCL Policy Lab and the Resolution Foundation.

Lawrence Sherman is Wolfson Professor Emeritus of Criminology at the University of Cambridge and Chief Scientific Officer for the Metropolitan Police. His research interests are in the fields of crime prevention, evidence-based policing, restorative justice, police practices and experimental criminology.

Robert Shiller is Sterling Professor of Economics at Yale University. He is also Professor of Finance and Fellow at the International Center for Finance at Yale School of Management. He was awarded the Nobel Prize in Economic Sciences jointly with Eugene Fama and Lars Peter Hansen in 2013. His latest book is *Narrative Economics: How Stories Go Viral and Drive Major Economic Events* (2019).

ABOUT THE PODCAST HOST

David Edmonds is a Consultant Researcher and Senior Research Associate at the Oxford Uehiro Centre for Practical Ethics. He runs the popular 'Philosophy Bites' podcast series with Nigel Warburton as well as 'Social Science Bites'. He is the bestselling author of *Wittgenstein's Poker* (2001) and his latest book, a biography of Derek Parfit called *Parfit: A Philosopher and His Mission to Save Morality*, was published by Princeton University Press in April 2023. He has written for outlets including the *Guardian*, *The Times*, *New Statesman*, *Prospect*, *Aeon*, the *Wall Street Journal* and the *Los Angeles Times*.

ABOUT THE PODCAST

In this series, which began in 2012, leading social and behavioural scientists share their perspectives on how our social world is created, and how these sciences can help us understand people and how they behave. Past guests include, in addition to this selection, President Biden's former deputy director for science and society, Alondra Nelson, world renowned cognitive scientist Steven Pinker, Nobel laureates Angus Deaton and Al Roth and pioneering geographer Doreen Massey.

Social Science Bites is produced in association with Sage, an independent, mission-driven academic publisher and the parent of Social Science Space (socialsciencespace.com), the home of Social Science Bites.

FOREWORD

If Ziyad Marar wasn't an insomniac, Social Science Bites would not exist. Sometime in early 2012, Ziyad, the president of global publishing at Sage, got in touch. At night, when he couldn't sleep, he'd been listening to Philosophy Bites, a podcast I made – and still make – with Nigel Warburton. Philosophy Bites has a big following among philosophers. Could we do for the social sciences, Ziyad wanted to know, what we'd done for philosophy?

Good question. We agreed to try – and since then Social Science Bites has been posting an interview at monthly intervals. There are now well over 100 and with an impressive roster of names.

And I love it. I have an excuse every month to talk to a leading thinker about a fascinating topic. We've covered everything from cities to religion, Weber to Durkheim, race inequalities and class inequalities, bias to disgust, happiness to death, ritual to sacred values, football to dance.

How do I select interviewees? Well, on the whole it's whatever takes my fancy, which for the listener has the advantage (or disadvantage) of resulting in what may seem a rather idiosyncratic miscellany. I suspect I have a bias towards the empirical, and I may be guilty of favouring quantitative over qualitative evidence (though Sam Friedman's work – see Chapter 1 – is a fine example of the importance of both). I try to keep an eye on disciplinary diversity: 'social science' is a broad category, with no fixed and settled boundaries, but core fields include economics, psychology, anthropology, sociology and political science.

In the past few years there has been an explosion in the number of podcasts available. There are podcasts on everything. If you're interested in cheese, you can find a podcast on cheese. Both Philosophy Bites and Social Science Bites were launched relatively early in this podcast revolution. My professional background is in radio, but podcasts have several advantages over traditional broadcasters. I'll mention just one. A radio programme has to be squeezed into an exact schedule. If the slot is 28 minutes, then that's how long the programme needs to be. That demands a procrustean approach: it might mean lengthening what should be a shorter programme, or cutting out material that one would ideally like to include. A podcast, by contrast, can be the duration it deserves to be.

The social science landscape has not changed as radically as the podcast one, but even during the lifetime of Social Science Bites I've noted a couple of intriguing trends. One is the increasing availability and use of data, which is transforming our understanding of how society functions. Perhaps related to this is the multidisciplinary nature of so much contemporary research; the anthropologist draws on psychology, the sociologist on economics, and so on. It's rarer, now, to find academics confined to subject silos. This is surely to be welcomed. After all, the philosophy underpinning Social Science Bites is that the social sciences have fundamental elements in common. They're on a branch of science that deals with complex human issues and problems, many of which are extremely tough to resolve.

This volume gives a flavour of what you can hear on the podcast. Obviously, we encourage you to go to Social Science Bites – hosted on Social Science Space and available on all the usual podcast platforms – where you can find many more interviews. They'll definitely keep you awake.

David Edmonds
(August, 2023)

IDENTITY

Sam Friedman
on
CLASS

Is education by itself the great equaliser? Will having the same education erase the benefit someone has from a higher class over someone from a lower class? Sociologist Sam Friedman, associate professor at the London School of Economics, says that education doesn't wash away the effects of class background. That doesn't deny that education has some role – and some successes – but he believes that education is not sufficient to unbinding the class system.

Listen to the podcast

https://www.socialsciencespace.com/2019/06/sam-friedman-on-class/

OCCUPATION VS A SET OF RESOURCES

There are two fairly dominant ways to think about social class in sociological terms. Perhaps the most dominant, and the one that's adopted by government and that we've used in our work most prominently here, is occupation. What sort of work do you do? What's the nature of that work, in terms of both your level of autonomy at work, as well as your sort of earnings potential? I think the other way of thinking about social class that we also use is that informed by the work of the French social theorist Pierre Bourdieu, which sees class as tied more to a set of resources that you have: economic, cultural, and also social.

The government's national socio-economic classification defines higher professional, managerial and administrative occupations. That's CEOs, doctors, academics, etc. We also wanted to slightly broaden the definition and include a set of cultural and creative professions. People working in film and television, actors, and other creative professions. Although these jobs perhaps don't have the same level of earnings compared to some of the traditional professions, they have an outsized cultural influence on the society that we live in, as well as being more competitive to access than our traditional top occupations.

CLASS AS ALLOCATION OF OPPORTUNITIES

We tend to think about the allocation of opportunities to these occupations as being bound to your educational credentials and your level of educational attainment. One of the key findings in our book is, both when you look at who is accessing these top occupations and also who's progressing in terms of these occupations, you see that those from privileged backgrounds have an advantage even when they have the same levels of educational credentials as those from working class backgrounds. In a way, that education doesn't wash away the effects of class background in terms of allocating opportunities. There are a lot of people who believe very strongly that these educational institutions can and do act as meritocratic sorting houses. They do to some extent. We need to be realistic and really look carefully at the evidence to see the limitations of that as an ideologically perfect way of allocating resources.

THE ENDURING ADVANTAGE OF A WEALTHY BACKGROUND

One of the profound drivers of the class pay gap is the enduring power that a wealthy background brings in terms of career advantages. We often think about the 'Bank of Mum and Dad', for example, as something that helps people get on the property ladder and afford certain lifestyle advantages. What we found is that the extent to which people draw upon those family sources of wealth is actually helping to build their careers. This is particularly the case in elite cultural and creative industries, where labour markets are very uncertain. We conducted about 175 interviews with people from a range of different top occupations, and we found that people from privileged backgrounds had relied upon this insulation that's provided by family wealth, to help them stay on that tightrope that helped them gain the requisite experience to then be considered for top roles. In contrast, what we found among people from working class backgrounds is that they often grudgingly self-selected out of the more creative or autonomous or prestigious areas of television or acting, for example, to go into areas such as admin, or marketing, where there was more stability and more security, but which didn't necessarily have the kind of career opportunities associated with these other pathways.

PUNCTURING THE MYTH OF CLASS

We're trying to puncture a myth that is incredibly powerful in British society, and more widely across most Western societies, which is that people not only want to believe but actually do believe that merit is the basis on which people progress. I think what we're trying to do here is show the limits of that understanding to show the ways in which we need to be very careful about banding around this idea of merit as an explanation for who gets ahead and, as a result, challenging the indi-vidualised explanations about why people succeed and fail. We tend to have this idea that people who do not achieve have some sort of deficit in their effort level, or culturally in terms of their value. I think in one way, we're trying to challenge that and get people to think more critically about meritocracy.

Janet Carsten

on

THE KINSHIP OF ANTHROPOLOGY.

The study of kinship, long the bread and butter of the anthropologist, has lost a bit of its centrality in the discipline. But as one of the leading exponents of what might be called the second coming of kinship studies, Janet Carsten, Professor of Social and Cultural Anthropology at the University of Edinburgh, has brought new blood into the field, exploring kinship's nexus with politics, work and gender.

Listen to the podcast

https://www.socialsciencespace.com/2016/01/janet-carsten-on-the-kinship-of-anthropology/

MORE THAN JUST FAMILY

Kinship for anthropologists includes all the social arrangements to do with what you might think of as family, but then, much more broadly, in classic anthropology it could include quite a lot to do with religion and political organisation because in many of the societies that anthropologists studied there were no states and so therefore the social organisation was very largely through kinship.

Blood is a symbol and perhaps one of the core symbols of kinship, but of course in not every culture is blood a very elaborated set of ideas. In European cultures blood is very important, and in many others too, but I wouldn't necessarily take that for granted. But also for anthropologists, kinship includes relations through marriage.

In many societies studied by anthropologists, the local religion – something like an ancestor cult – includes relations with elders, people who are older than you, but also the dead in classic Chinese religion was like that. So those are called ancestor cults usually in anthropology, but they come out of a much broader set of kinship relations. Similarly, in the societies that mid-twentieth century British social anthropologists studied, political organisation in the absence of states was through kinship. So they were primarily interested in kinship for that religious and political dimension it gave to society, for the way that it organised society in the absence of states rather than in the close familial domestic relations which we might think of as kinship.

KINSHIP IS UNIVERSAL

Kinship is universal in the sense that it is at the core of every society. But the way kinship is organised varies from culture to culture, and although you can group those cultures and say this one is unilineal, another is bilateral, and so on, and there are various typologies for doing that, it's also the case that kinship organisation is both universal and variable – in the sense, for example, that people have different rules about who you are not allowed to have sex with.

From the 1970s onwards, kinship lost its centrality partly because it became a rather abstract, dry and technical subject and lots of people couldn't quite understand the point. But also, anthropology moved on and there was an interest in postcolonialism, so in the political evolution of postcolonial societies. And to some extent, the place of kinship was partly taken by the feminist upsurge outside the academy as well as within it, which meant that there was a very strong interest in gender relations. Obviously, gender and kinship have overlapped in the way anthropologists have studied it, and many have argued that you can't understand gender without understanding kinship. So there was much more overt interest in the study of gender, and to some extent kinship seemed rather marginal. But I think it's moved on in all sorts of interesting ways, and perhaps more recently become more interesting again because there've been various rather specific inputs – interests in reproductive technologies, for example, and what they do to kinship relations. But also the idea that kinship is marginal might itself be a reflection of the stories we tell ourselves about modernity. In other words, that in 'modern' societies, kinship is relegated to the nuclear family, to the family domain, and domestic relations, and doesn't really have anything to do with politics or religion.

IT'S ABOUT PEOPLE'S EVERYDAY LIVES

Kinship is not a kind of abstract and technical subject – or it doesn't have to be like that. It's really about people's everyday lives and the way they think about the relations that matter most to them. And so for most people, if you think about their imaginative lives – quite a big part of what occupies people, what preoccupies them – is actually their family relations, thinking about that in the broadest sense. That is, how they're connected to the people that really matter to them. We might include close friendship there. So people spend an enormous amount of time and effort doing things and thinking about their close relationships, and I'm always interested in how that works and also in how it plays out over time between generations, why commemorating kinship relations matters, and what memory and kinship do together. So, the kind of everyday stuff of kinship is what interests me. The criticism that one might make of that is that it's very specific, and how do you get back to the kind of broad questions that someone like Lévi-Strauss was much more interested in? But I think it's partly through showing some quite nitty-gritty stuff on the ground that you are able to draw that out and think well, why does this matter? And that's a question that anthropologists should always be asking themselves. Why is this important? What does it tell us about society more generally?

HOW WE THINK AND LEARN

ABOUT THIS PODCAST

Thinking is hard, and most of the time we rely on simple psychological mechanisms that can lead us astray. Nobel Prize-winning psychologist Daniel Kahneman, Professor of Psychology and Public Affairs Emeritus at Princeton University, and author of *Thinking, Fast and Slow*, talks to Nigel Warburton about biases in our reasoning. His research has revealed that human beings are not the rational decision-makers that many economists had claimed they were.

Listen to the podcast

https://www.socialsciencespace.com/2013/01/daniel-kahneman-on-bias/

THINKING FAST AND THINKING SLOW

When I say '2 + 2', the number 4 comes to mind, and when I say '17 x 24', nothing comes immediately to mind – you are generally aware that this is a multiplication problem. The first kind of thinking, which I associate with System 1, is completely associative, it just happens to you, a thought comes to mind as it were spontaneously or automatically. The second kind of thinking, the one that would produce an answer to the question by computation: that is serial, that is effortful. That is why I call it System 2 or slow thinking.

System 1 is defined really as anything that happens automatically in the mind that is without any sense of effort, and usually without a sense of authorship. It is something that happens to you, it isn't something you do. In some cases it could even be an intention: a wish to do something which you feel is something that happens to you.

Now the domain of System 2 is that when we speak about System 2, we speak about effortful thinking, and that includes not only computation and reasoning, but it also includes self-control. Self-control is effortful. And so anything that demands mental effort tends to be classified as System 2 or slow thinking.

This is more of a metaphor to describe how the brain works, or the mind works. What happens to us, what we do, and how we think involves both systems almost always. System 1, I propose, is invariably active: ideas and thoughts and emotions come to mind through an associative process all the time. And System 2 has a control function: we don't say anything that comes to mind, and it has in addition to the computational function, the ability to inhibit thoughts from being expressed; it controls action and that is effortful. It's the interaction between System 1 and System 2 that, in effect – in the story that I tell – defines who we are and how we think.

AUTOMATIC – SYSTEM 1 – THINKING

One characteristic of System 1 or automatic thinking is that something comes to your mind almost always – appropriate or not. Whenever you're faced with a question or a challenge, very likely something will come to your mind. Quite often what comes to your mind is not an answer to the question that you were trying to answer, but it's an answer to another question, a different question. This happens all the time: I ask you how probable something is and instead of probability, what comes to your mind is that you can think of many instances, and you will rely on that to answer the probability question; and it is that substitution that produces systematic biases.

We rely on systematic thinking much less than we think we do. Much of the time when we think we are thinking systematically; that is, when we think we have a reason for our conclusions. In effect the conclusions are dictated by the associative machinery. They are conclusions produced by System 1, in my terminology, which are then rationalised by System 2. So much of our thinking involves System 2 producing explanations for intuitions or feelings that arose automatically in System 1.

WHY DON'T WE USE SYSTEM 2 MORE?

Because it's hard work. A law of least effort applies. People are reluctant; some more than others, there are large individual differences. But thinking is hard, and it's also slow. Because automatic thinking is usually so efficient, and usually so successful, we have very little reason to work very hard mentally. And frequently we don't work hard when, if we did, we would reach different conclusions.

As a society, when we provide education, we are strengthening System 2; when we teach people that reasoning logically is a good thing we are strengthening System 2. It is not going to make people completely rational, or make people completely reasonable, but you can work in that direction, and certainly self-control is variable. Some people have much more of it than other people, and all of us exert self-control more in some situations than in others. And so creating conditions under which people are less likely to abandon self-control is part of promoting rationality. We are never going to get there, but we can move in that direction.

People are interested in promoting rational behaviour. They can be helped, I presume, by analysing the obstacles to rational, reasonable behaviour, and trying to get around those obstacles.

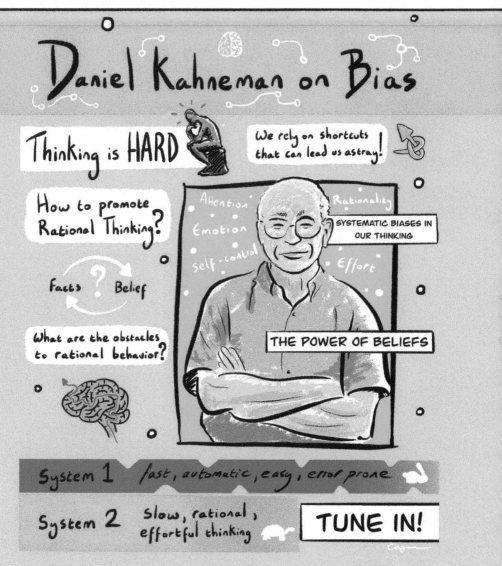

Mahzarin Banaji
on
IMPLICIT BIAS

There's probably no more famous and influential test in psychology than the Implicit Association Test. It's an ingenious way of trying to get at our implicit bias. We might, for example, explicitly reject racism but at some sort of unconscious level, we could still harbour prejudiced thoughts and assumptions. The test is available online and has been taken by millions of people. It has helped make the concept of implicit bias common place. Mahzarin Banaji, Professor of Social Ethics at Harvard University, explains her work on implicit bias and the efforts she and her colleagues made in creating the Implicit Association Test.

Listen to the podcast

THE THUMBPRINT OF CULTURE ON OUR BRAIN

Implicit bias is a way to get at the thumbprint of the culture on our brain. We walk through life, learning things, and seeing things, and putting things together. From the time I'm a child as I walk down the street, I see who the poor people are and who the rich people are, and where one lives and where the other lives. My brain puts things together that repeatedly get paired in our experience. Implicit bias is just another word for capturing what those are.

PREJUDICE IS A CONSCIOUS ACT

Prejudice is a very conscious act. When I say something like, 'This particular group of people, they're all just lazy'. That's an example of a prejudice. But as we know, with every decade in the last century, these biases have been going away. Explicit statements of prejudice are less and less to be found, and I see that as a mark of progress. I see that as people saying, 'I don't wish to think that way'. But our data shows that when you use tests to get a little bit below the surface, what you see is that, even though you might reject an explicit bias, you actually have the implicit version of it.

If you're a white American, the likelihood is that if you're part of the majority, you will to some extent find it easier to associate white with good and black with bad. What's surprising about this is that you're a person who harbours no conscious race bias: racism is when you say consciously, 'I think black people aren't deserving of X, Y, or Z', or that they're less intelligent. What the test picks up is the roots of prejudice. We've been talking about skin colour, but there are tests for a variety of things such as gender, body size, age, and sexuality.

WILL IMPLICIT BIAS TRAINING SUCCEED?

I don't believe implicit bias training is going to be very successful, because I just don't believe that most people are going to think that they should correct it, or know how to correct it. But do I think, theoretically, it's possible? Absolutely. There are many people I've talked to who have drastically changed the way in which they make their own decisions, because of coming face-to-face with the data from their own test results.

BIAS IS CREATED VERY FAST

We are born with a machine that learns very fast: it learns to create a bias very fast. Black is bad, and white is good, or gay is dirty and straight is good, or female cooks and male goes to the office. These are all absolutely learned. But the machine that learns them is so powerful, and so ready to learn, that we have been surprised how early children show evidence of implicit bias. So many years ago, we created a child version of the IAT, which is very much like the adult version, except that kids wear headphones and we present a lot of the stimuli auditorily. We play words like 'yucky' and 'nice' in their ear, and they press a key. They love these tests because it's a game they feel they have to beat. When we administered the test, and we had groups of six-year-olds, ten-year-olds and adults, the ten-year-olds came out looking identical to the adults, and we thought that might happen. Then the six-year-olds looked identical to the adults, so we were actually surprised. Now we've developed some tests where we can show that by age three, children are looking pretty much the same as adults.

HOW MUCH DO YOU LIKE THE OTHER?

Going into the research, we had 100 years of research, where people were asked the question, how much do you like your group? How much do you like the other? Britain is well known for a series of experiments and a theory called social identity theory, the idea being that our groups are so important to us that we will kill for our group. You will prefer your own to another; you will divide resources in such a way that your group benefits over the other end. We expect to see that white likes white and black likes black, that young likes young and elderly likes elderly. But that result depends greatly on where your group sits in the social hierarchy. If you come from a dominant group – if you're straight, if you're young, if you're white – there's a preference for your own. But if you come from the less advantaged end of these groups – you're elderly, you're African American, you're gay – you don't show the same degree of group love.

Gurminder K. Bhambra
on
POSTCOLONIAL SOCIAL SCIENCE

How much do you know about the Haitian Revolution of the late 18th/early 19th century? You'll almost certainly have more knowledge of the French Revolution. Former empires conveniently forget the contributions of their colonies now that these colonies have downgraded to mere 'nations'. There are lessons to learn with the current impulse to pull down statues, explains Gurminder K. Bhambra, sociologist and professor in the School of Global Studies at the University of Sussex.

Listen to the podcast

https://www.socialsciencespace.com/2020/07/gurminder-k-bhambra-on-postcolonial-social-science/

THE DEEP ORIGINS OF POSTCOLONIAL STUDIES

Postcolonialism is a field that emerged within academia in the 1980s, and one of its touchstone texts is the book *Orientalism* by Edward Said, which was published in 1978. It was so influential initially within English literature, but then within the humanities more generally, that it built up a body of scholarship in its wake. That came to be understood as postcolonial studies.

When we look at the Declaration of the Rights of Man and the Citizen that emerged out of the French Revolution, one of the things that for me was significant was to see that there was a clause in there for the abolition of slavery. The abolition of slavery is one of the most radical proposals of that declaration. What's interesting to know is the only reason that clause was there was because a group of people who had liberated themselves from slavery in St. Domingue, which comes to be known as Haiti, had traveled across the Atlantic to the Constituent Assembly in the 1790s, to argue for the abolition of slavery. The fact that in 1794 the abolition of slavery within the Declaration of the Rights of Man and the Citizen, is only there as a consequence of formerly enslaved Africans who had liberated themselves through the Haitian Revolution, traveling across the Atlantic, and putting it there. To know this transforms our understanding of human rights away from something that is seen to be a European phenomenon that's then given to the rest of the world. It causes us to think about the ways in which those histories of colonisation and imperialism are actually the basis for the emergence of some of the most radical ideas and initiatives that we falsely give over simply to a European legacy.

TAKING THE HAITIAN REVOLUTION SERIOUSLY

Historians have often engaged with Haiti, but social scientists haven't. When social scientists talk about the emergence of democracy and think about modern politics, they always go to the French Revolution and the American Revolution. Very rarely is the Haitian Revolution central to their understandings. Part of the difficulty for people is that if we were to take Haiti seriously, we would have to call into question the value that we otherwise assert to the American and French revolutions. Because remember, Haiti had been a colony of France, and both France and the US continued to maintain slavery, within the colonies for France and across the continent in the US. And they continued to maintain segregated forms of political life, at least till the 1960s, in the US and in France, until Algeria gained independence in the early 1960s. Both countries that are presented as the foundation of democracy are slave societies, are colonial societies, are societies that maintain segregation, and denied the equality of all humans up until the late 20th century. If we took Haiti seriously, it would force us to confront this contradiction between the ideals of America and France and their very real practices.

BRITAIN AND THE NATIONAL PROJECT

In the context of the Brexit referendum that we had in 2016, the debates around that time were very much around reclaiming our sovereignty and national sovereignty. There was this sense that what we wished to do was to reconstitute ourselves as a nation with a national past. But our past in Britain is not a national past. It's an imperial past. Britain has never actually been a nation. Britain only came into being in 1707, when there was the union of the kingdoms of England and Scotland. Both England and Scotland at that time had colonies in the Americas but also closer to home. The relationship to Ireland is a complex one, but you could see the way in which Ireland itself was part of this colonial matrix. Then together, they went on to establish an empire, which by the 1920s, covered about one-fifth of the world's population. The British Empire was always a multicultural entity and it continued in existence until 1948, when it was transformed into the Commonwealth. Then in 1973, we entered the European Economic Community. At no point in the history of Britain, has Britain been a nation; there may well have been a national project, but the state was always an imperial state.

MAKING HISTORY BETTER UNDERSTOOD

I want history to be better understood. I would wish the history curriculum to have British Empire as a compulsory module. At the moment, school kids don't have to learn about the British Empire: the only topic that is compulsory within the national curriculum for history is the Holocaust. I think it's incredibly important that students are taught about the Second World War, and the Holocaust. I think it's important for British school kids to understand British history. You cannot understand British history without understanding it as a colonial and imperial history.

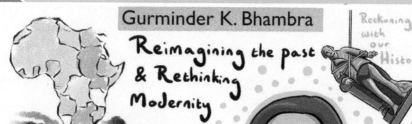

Jonathan Haidt on

MORAL PSYCHOLOGY

ABOUT THIS PODCAST

Abortion, capital punishment, euthanasia, free speech, marriage, homosexuality: topics on which liberals and conservatives take radically different views. But why do we adopt certain moral and political judgements? Jonathan Haidt, a social psychologist, was formerly a staunch liberal. His research has now convinced him that no one political persuasion has a monopoly on the truth. Jonathan Haidt is Professor of Ethical Leadership at New York University. In this podcast he discusses the place of rationality in our moral judgements.

Listen to the podcast

https://www.socialsciencespace.com/2012/10/jonathan-haidt-on-moral-psychology/

WHAT WE OUGHT TO DO VS WHAT WE ACTUALLY DO

Philosophers are certainly licensed to help us think about what we ought to do, but what we actually do is the domain of psychologists, and just as you can talk about a linguistic psychologist, or sexual psychologist, we study all different aspects of human nature: morality, moral judgement, moral behaviour, hypocrisy, righteousness. These are major, major topics of huge importance to our political lives, and our common lives.

It involves the use of scientific methods which don't have to be experimental: we can do observation and correlation. As with any difficult area to study, you want to use a lot of different methods, and there's no substitute for tuning up your own intuitions, for doing some field work, for reading widely, for talking to people who have varying moral world views. So, in that sense it can be a little bit like anthropology.

IT'S IN THE BRAIN

The short thing to say about it is 'Wow, it's in the brain, the brain actually makes us do moral judgements'. The more interesting thing to say about it is 'Huh! Look at which areas of the brain are particularly active'. The fact that we reason logically, we feel emotions, the insula fires when we're disgusted. I'm on the side that says the two different emotional reactions tend to drive the reasoning reactions, and I think most of the neuroscience literature is consistent with that.

WHAT CONSTRAINS OUR MORALITY, LIKE POLITICS

For the most part, we are constrained when we are doing moral reasoning about anything that is vaguely relevant to us. Some people think that I deny that rationality exists, and no, not at all. You know, we're able to reason about all sorts of things. I mean, if I want to get from point A to point B, I'll figure it out, and then if somebody gives me a counterargument and shows me that, no, it's faster to go through C, I'll believe him. But moral judgements aren't just about what's going on in the world. Our morality is constrained by so many factors; one of the main ones is our team membership. And so political disagreements have a rather notorious history of being completely impervious to reasons given by the other side, which then makes the other side think that we are not sincere, we're not rational, and both sides think that about each other. Because what you think about abortion, gay rights, whether a single mother is as good as a married couple as parents, all of these things tie you to your team, and if you change your mind, you are now a traitor, you will not be invited to dinner parties and you might be called some nasty names.

DOING EXPERIMENTS TO MANIPULATE INTUITIONS

My own research involved giving people scenarios that were disgusting, or disrespectful, but had no harm – things like a family that eats their pet dog after the dog was killed by a car in front of their house. On that scenario, the Ivy League undergraduates did generally say that it was OK; if they chose to do that, it was OK. So there was one group that was rational utilitarian in that sense, or rights-based I suppose you would also say. But the great majority of people, especially in Brazil and especially working-class in both countries, said 'No, it's wrong, it's disrespectful, there's more to morality.' So just descriptively most people have a lot of moral intuitions: they're not utilitarians. When you interview them about these, or if you do experiments where you manipulate intuitions, you can basically drive their reasoning to follow the intuitions.

STUDYING MORALITY IN SOCIAL SCIENCE

If you're studying morality, it's kind of like you're studying the operating system of our social life. And since the operating system of academe is very liberal, I was enmeshed in the liberal team; and as I said, my goal here was to help my team win. I wasn't trying to pervert my science, but I was trying to use it as an activist would. We have a lot of debate in social psychology as to whether it's OK to be activist, because we have a lot of social psychologists who are activists especially on race and gender issues, and most people think that's OK. But I've come to think it's not. Once you become part of a team, motivated reasoning and the confirmation bias are so powerful that you're going to find support for whatever you want to believe. I mean, I'd like to think that my research, eventually, helped me get out of my team and be a free agent.

Some people are lucky, they're just born good at maths. And those who aren't will never be able to compete, however well they're taught. We all know that, except, according to Jo Boaler, professor at Stanford University, it's not true.
In fact, pretty much everything you think about math education turns out to be a myth.

Listen to
the podcast

https://www.socialsciencespace.com/2018/01/jo-boaler-fear-mathematics/

NO SUCH THING AS MATH BRAIN

The neuroscience is showing us pretty clearly that there's no such thing as a math brain, even though so many people believe that, particularly the Western culture. What we know from neuroscience is that mathematical pathways grow in the brain; they grow when you learn something. The first time we learn something, a tiny, delicate little pathway forms. That idea becomes deeper and deeper until it's a permanent brain pathway. We're not born with those pathways, they come about when we learn things. What the neuroscience is telling us is that every moment of your life, every second, you have experiences where brain pathways can begin to grow and deepen. By the time children are three or four years old, they've had many different experiences that have grown different pathways. You can have two eight-year-old children who are completely different, one of whom finds maths easy, and one who finds it very difficult. That's much more likely to be because of all the different networks that have developed in their brains.

WHO DOES BETTER IN STANDARDISED TESTS?

In my research, I have contrasted students working in different ways; there's a lot of contention and we have a lot of ideas about what's good in maths. So, I decided to study it. I followed hundreds of students over many years, some of whom have sat in rows, listening to a teacher lecture, and then repeating exercises. And others of which have actively explored with mathematical ideas, being much more actively involved, applying methods, working on challenging problems. The kids who are more actively involved in their learning did a lot better in standardised tests.

THE TIMES TABLE ISSUE

The times tables by-rote issue is a very big issue because many of us did that. We memorise times tables. It turns out, you don't need to do that. It's much better to have a really strong number sense, which you don't get from memorising times tables; rather you get this from really working conceptually with numbers. In general, kids learning by rote learning, by memory, do not do as well as kids who are thinking hard and conceptually about mathematics.

WHAT NEEDS TO CHANGE IN MATH EDUCATION?

There's so much that needs to change in math education. One of the things is lots of kids are sitting there thinking, 'I don't have a math brain'. Then when they make a mistake, that's more evidence that they don't have a math brain. It's actually really productive to make a mistake. The best times for brain growth are when your brain is struggling and when you're making mistakes.

We know that timed tests inhibit the brain from working. One of the recent findings is that when people feel anxious, and if you put a math test in front of someone in a timed position, they start to feel anxious, the working memory in the brain becomes compromised. If you need to recall math facts, you need your working memory. The worst thing we can do with little kids is give them timed math tests. In the US where I work, people have seen this brain research and they're pulling timed tests out of schools and out of districts.

Assessment is good and helpful for students, teachers, all sorts of people. Math should not be a speed race. One of the things that we advocate for is dissociating math from speed altogether. This is another damaging myth that people have: to be good at math, you have to be fast at math. Turns out that's not true. In fact, a lot of the world's greatest mathematicians will tell you they're very slow. With math, they need to think deeply, and they can't work fast. They don't do well on timed tests. So dissociating maximum speed is very important. We can assess students, and good teachers are assessing their students all the time; they know how well students are doing.

BOYS DON'T DO BETTER AT MATH

If you look at school performance, boys don't do better than girls at math. In the recent PISA international math tests, boys did better than girls in 34 countries. When they factored in anxiety, that gender difference went away completely. This tells us that girls are more anxious in math tests than boys and that undermines their performance. Math is important for everyone, but we really should be changing the kind of math we do with kids in school.

SOCIAL SCIENCE BITES PRESENTS...
Fear of Mathematics
Everything you know about Maths education is Wrong!
Jo Boaler
There is no 'Maths brain'
New Pathways form as we Learn!
Any child can excel
ANXIETY FEAR DOUBT
"MATH WARS"
Don't make SPEED a factor
How best to teach maths?
Memorisation vs Active Learning
(this one's best!)
NEGATIVE EXPERIENCES
Too Much testing!!!!!
TEST
It's good to make mistakes mistakes → It's how we GROW
Constant Measuring does not make us grow any taller
Have a Growth MINDSET
TUNE IN!

Saskia Sassen

on

BEFORE METHOD

Saskia Sassen is a sociologist who was born in the Netherlands and raised and educated around the world. That might be one biographical explanation for how she's been able to bring a critical eye on existing ways of framing social phenomena. She's coined a phrase to describe her approach: 'before method'. Known for her concept of the 'global city', she is Co-Director of Columbia University's Committee on Global Thought.

Listen to the podcast

https://www.socialsciencespace.com/2014/05/saskia-sassen-on-before-method/

THIS EPISTEMIC INDIGNATION

'Before method' really was shaped by two things: one is how I do research, how I wind up wanting to explore a certain subject. The second part harkens back a bit to Kafka's 'Before the Law': before the law being the space either of fear (because the law is about to come down and chop off your head), or the space of epistemic indignation, an indignation that is mental: the mental violence that you experience when authoritative explanation is wrong. I have that with a lot of the neo-liberal explanations about where we're at in our world today. So, between those two elements I realise that I'm really in this epistemic indignation, and because I'm in that zone, I need freedom and flexibility to position myself vis-à-vis my object of study in whatever way I want. So 'before method' is that space before I need to enter the disciplining of method in the conventional social sciences.

BEING ALERT TO POWERFUL EXPLANATIONS

Since I was a very junior scholar I have always been on alert vis-à-vis powerful explanations, categories for analysis, that presume to be able to capture the critical elements of a condition. Maybe it's because I grew up in Latin America, then I was raised in Italy and in France, then I came to the United States. I have traveled across all sorts of epistemic domains also in terms of how people explain something. It's not a beating-your-chest kind of violence that you feel, it's really mental, and it becomes a mental project and hence it becomes a knowledge-making project.

ANALYTIC TACTICS

I developed what I like to think of as analytic tactics – not analytic strategies – analytic *tactics*: in other words, very instrumental, little steps. One issue for me has become that when I invoke a powerful explanation, I am invoking something which is collectively produced over time that really does explain, that has been subjected to analyses and contestation, and that has survived all of that. It is powerful. So I cannot just throw it out of the window, but what I can do is ask, 'When I invoke this category, what *don't* I see?' Now, in so far as I'm working in a period that I think of as one where stable meanings are becoming unstable, what does it mean today to say 'the economy', or 'the national economy'? What does it mean to say 'the middle classes'? What does it mean to say 'the nation state'? What does it mean to say 'unemployment'? Et cetera, et cetera. I find all of these right now are slightly unstable, if not sharply unstable in some cases, so then it becomes valid or to ask, 'If I invoke these powerful categories, what don't I see?' In the most extreme version of all of this I would say that they are so full of meaning, these powerful categories, that they function as an invitation not to think.

FORGET THE CATEGORY: GO AND SEE WHAT YOU SEE

My first book, which is now considered a classic, *The Mobility of Labour and Capital*, was rejected by 12 publishers. I kept sending it. I violated all the rules of the game. At one point I sent seven to seven publishers. I kept going at it. I was running out of publishers, by the way. The thirteenth took it. I believed in that book and I never changed a sentence. I think there my foreignness has given me a third point of view that fits neither here nor there, literally. That is my own zone of combat, and now I'm giving it a name, 'before method'. When I do research on immigration, I suspend the category. And I tell my students, 'If you're going to do research on immigration, forget the category "immigration" exists: go see what you see.' I did the same thing with globalisation; I had to get rid of it otherwise it just leads you in a different direction. Now most people have done fine being led by that category. I'm not saying nobody should be doing it because it thankfully allows me to do what I do. There is a lot of content in that category today.

SOCIAL SCIENCE BITES PRESENTS...
SASKIA SASSEN
BEFORE METHOD
Dealing with Epistemic Resignation
We live in a world of Categories
'De-theorise'
Return to ground level
What is the Key Conceptual Category?
Post Modernism
The Global City
Place still matters
Suspend the Category!
Observe
Don't be led astray by Categories
A 3rd View: Before Method
TUNE IN!

HUMAN
BEHAVIOUR

Stephen Reicher
on

CROWD
PSYCHOLOGY

We know that groups can be dangerous. Mob-mentality takes over, and ordinary people become capable of terrible things, right? But is the psychology of group behaviour as straightforward as that? Steve Reicher, psychologist and professor at St Andrews University, in Scotland, has done extensive research on how people behave collectively. He has a more nuanced and more optimistic view, a view that includes the possibility that group mentality can bring out the best in us, as well as the worst.

Listen to the podcast

https://www.socialsciencespace.com/2016/02/stephen-reicher-on-crowd-psychology/

WHAT GROUPS HAVE TO SAY ABOUT HUMAN SOCIALITY

I've been very interested in the psychology of groups, how we behave in groups, how we are transformed by groups, and what groups have to say about the nature of human sociality. At the same time, I've been really interested in groups as a source of change, a source of resistance; in a sense, you could summarise the literature as saying 'groups are bad for you'.

Groups take rational individuals, they take moral individuals, and they turn them into immoral idiots, and I've been trying to contest that notion, but also to explain how that notion comes about.

GROUPS: HUNDREDS OF YOU CRAMMED IN

We are socialists, we are Catholics, whatever it might be, and the best way of illustrating that is through an experience which anybody, certainly who lives in London, will have had: you're in that Underground or Overground carriage, and you're part of a physical group. There are hundreds of you crammed in, but you feel no psychological commonality. You're psychologically individual; if anybody looks over your shoulder at your newspaper you feel violated. If they brush up against you, it makes you shudder.

But then the train breaks down, and there's one of the countless excuses from that huge book of excuses — the wrong type of leaves or snow, whatever it might be — and then things change, because then you get an emergent sense of commonality. We are aggrieved commuters, by contrast with the company. We form a category, and you see people begin to turn to each other, talk to each other, even sometimes share their sandwiches, which, as British people, is really extreme. So you can see we all have that experience of the transition from the physical to a psychological group, where people have, if you like, that sense of 'we'.

THE BOUNDARIES OF 'WE' AND 'THEY'

Not only can it form very quickly, but it also shows us that the boundaries of 'we' and 'they' are almost infinitely malleable and change as part of a social process. So one of the key aspects, I think, of contemporary group psychology is an insistence on what one might call the 'variable self'; the fact that one can move from an individual self to a collective self very quickly, but also the fact that the boundaries of selfhood can change very quickly, as well.

One of the things we've been studying for many years is the escalation of violence. The problem with the classic psychology, which says all groups are dangerous and that says even reasonable people can get carried away in the crowd is, it suggests, in particular when trouble starts in a crowd, that everybody might become involved, everybody is equally dangerous, and therefore leads to practices of intervention which clamp down on everyone.

WE NEED TO LOOK AT INTERGROUP INTERACTIONS

Now, we argue that, first of all, when you have intergroup violence, it's almost impossible to explain it by just looking at one party to that violence, just looking at the crowd. We need to look at the intergroup interactions, the intergroup dynamics between crowd and police. Second, in a number of very different types of crowd events – student demonstrations, environmentalist disputes, and so on – you can see a common dynamic of escalation, whereby you get an initially heterogeneous crowd, in which some people want to do more confrontational things, but most people don't, then trouble starts, so the police see them all as dangerous and clamp down on everyone. Then people who didn't previously see themselves as anti-police are being treated as the opposition, so see themselves as oppositional, and therefore you see a shift and an escalation.

THE REAL ISSUE ABOUT CROWD BEHAVIOUR

The real issue about crowd behaviour and crowd violence isn't why a few people who came to be violent are violent – that's a rather banal issue – it's why so many people who came not to be violent, become involved in those dynamics, those dynamics of escalation. Now, that's a tough message to get through because, of course, when there is trouble, the *first* thing any government wants to do is to admit that it, its policies, or its agencies might play a role in the creation of that conflict; that the police don't just manage and control violence, they might be a party to the creation and construction of violence. On the other hand, of course, actually it's a very practical form of theory, and it begins to point to very clear forms of intervention and different forms of policing. We've talked about facilitative policing: policing which starts off by asking what are the groups in the crowd? What are their different identities and intentions, which ones can we facilitate? And if the police start from asking not 'What can we stop?' but 'What can we allow and how can we help people?', then you get a very different set of dynamics.

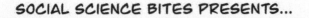

Crowd Psychology

Stephen Reicher

Reconsidering Groups

The MAD MOB view

Groups as IRRATIONAL & IMMORAL

This view protects the Status Quo from challenge

We pathologize groups

Only in the crowd do we become the subjects of history

But LISTEN CHANGE

Groups give Power to the Powerless

We don't lose agency in groups, we GAIN it!

Indiscriminate responses by authorities ESCALATE VIOLENCE

TUNE IN!

Robert Shiller
on
BEHAVIOURAL ECONOMICS

In the past 20 years there has been a revolution in economics with the study not of how people would behave if they were perfectly rational, but of how they actually behave. At the vanguard of this movement is Robert Shiller, Professor of Economics at Yale University.

Listen to the podcast

https://www.socialsciencespace.com/2012/08/robert-shiller-on-behavioral-economics/

The word 'behavioural' refers to the introduction of other social sciences into economics: psychology, sociology, and political science. It's a revolution in economics that has taken place over the past 20 years or so. I think it's bringing economics into a broader appreciation of reality. Economics was actually more behavioural 50 or 100 years ago. At Yale University where I work, 1927 was the year where the department of economics, sociology and government was split into three separate departments and they moved us all apart.

There are both advantages and disadvantages of this structure. The advantage is that we develop mathematical economics and mathematical finance to a very advanced level – and it's useful: we have option pricing theory that is very subtle and allows complex calculations that have some relevance to understanding these markets. But it loses perspective on why we have these options anyway. It offers a justification typically that involves rational behaviour. You can get into the swim of that, thinking 'I want to know why smart people use options'. And it's instructive to go through the exercise of thinking 'Is it really ever right to buy these investment products?' But that doesn't mean that you're answering the question why people *really* do buy options and why this market exists and why other markets that sound equally plausible don't exist.

Conventional economics misrepresents what our best interests are. A great example is the financial crisis that began in 2007. The way it began is home prices started falling rapidly. Many people had committed themselves to mortgages and now the debt was worth more than the house was worth, they couldn't come up with the money to pay off the mortgage and so it kind of led to a world financial crisis. So why did that happen? Conventional economic theory can't seem to get at the answer, which I would say is, we had a speculative bubble driven by excessive optimism, driven by public inattention to risks of such an eventuality. And errors in managing the mortgage contracts were made. There are no errors in conventional economics: it's all rational optimisation.

Economic theory likes to reduce human behaviour to a canonical form. The structure has been, ever since Samuelson wrote this a half century ago, that people want to maximise their consumption. All they want to do is consume goods; they don't care about anyone else. There's neither benevolence nor malevolence. All they care about is eating or getting goods and they want to smooth it: they described it in terms of so-called utility functions through their lifetime and that's it. That is such an elegant, simple model, but it's too simple. And if you look at what psychology shows, the mind is the product of human evolution and it has lots of different patterns of behaviour. The discoveries that psychologists make to economics are manifold.

A sense of fairness is a fundamental human universal. It's been found in some recent studies that it even goes beyond humans, that higher primates do have some vestigial or limited understanding of fairness and equity. In terms of how the market responds to crises, economists assume that everything is done purely out of self-interest. And yet non-economists – when we ask them about how things work – have a totally different view.

Economists just sometimes don't see the obvious, they don't rely on mental faculties of human judgement that they have, as well as not relying on a broader view of people that's informed by psychological or sociological research.

I think that the economics profession suffers from physics-envy. I really do. We all wish we could be Einstein. It's too strong a model; we can't all develop the theory of relativity. The world of people isn't like that. When you look at what happens for example in a financial crisis, you've got to get immersed in a lot of detail. It doesn't become understandable by abstract economic reasoning. This means you have to look at an impression of what's driving people, what's on their minds, what they don't know, what the lawyers did with the contracts, what the people are assuming the government might do if such and such happens. It involves a lot of real-world thinking that doesn't fit with the Einstein model.

Robert Shiller on

Importance of framing

Danger of Oversimplified models

Behavioral Economics

Economics strives for the certainties of physics

But humans are Messy...

Insights from neuroscience

Neuroeconomics

The Fallacy of the Rational Individual

TUNE IN!

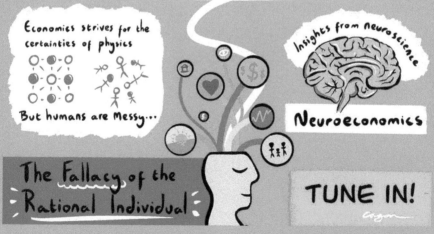

David Halpern
on
NUDGING

Placing more nutritious food on a more visible shelf, informing lagging taxpayers that their neighbours have already paid up, or asking job seekers what they plan to do next week (instead of what they did – or didn't do – last week) – these are all well-known examples of behavioural spurs known as 'nudges'. Much of the reason such examples are known is because they emanate from the work of the Behavioural Insights Team – the so-called nudge unit, set up by the United Kingdom's government. Experimental psychologist David Halpern, the unit's chief executive, has led the team since its inception.

Listen to the podcast

https://www.socialsciencespace.com/2019/01/david-halpern-on-nudging/

LEVERS OF HUMAN BEHAVIOUR

The Behavioural Insights Team was set up in British government in 2010, a unit to try and use more realistic models of human behaviour to see if we could solve both big and small problems in government. Our prime focus is social problems and government policy. Our prime concern is not to help one company beat another, but try and solve climate change or get people to pay their tax on time.

The sense was that there are a whole lot of other levers that we could use and other factors that drive human behaviour that aren't really captured in traditional policy leavers. It's called the 'Nudge Unit'. It seems to me that 'nudge' has never been clearly defined. It's not obvious what a nudge is. We take a slightly broader perspective, which is trying to introduce a more realistic model of human behaviour. A nudge, as defined on the North American side, is a more realistic model of human behaviour. This rests on the idea that the human is not entirely rational, that we're driven by all sorts of impulses. We're driven by emotion.

People are really busy, and they've got other things to do in their lives, a lot of stuff you have to process all at once. We tend to use mental shortcuts to figure out what's going on. Most of the time, those mental shortcuts actually get us to where we want to go, but they are subject to systematic error.

NUDGING WITH JOBSEEKERS

We ran trials, on the back of noticing that many jobseekers didn't turn up for interviews or opportunities for work. Some job centres would then send people a little prompt. We ran more elaborate versions of that and we found that if you send someone a text saying 'Dave, don't forget your interview' – if you put the other person's name on it and add something a little bit human – we would find that nearly three times more people will turn up at that interview. It's quite a fundamental shift in some ways, which is away from a system built on a lack of trust. It makes people much more likely to then follow through and get a job faster. The beauty of it is it also works most effectively for the people who are most disorganised in their job search.

TRUST EXERCISES

In countries like the UK and the US, typically, about 30–35% of people say most others can be trusted. In places like Sweden however, you'd get 60–70% of people say most others can be trusted. If you go to Latin America, or Africa, it will be less than 10%. These are massive differences and are incredibly consequential. There are also massive social class differences on both sides of the Atlantic, so people who come from poor backgrounds, low income backgrounds, essentially disadvantaged in various ways, tend to have much lower levels of social trust and more impoverished social networks than people who come from more affluent backgrounds.

Within Britain, we have National Citizen Service, which is an opportunity for young people at 16–17 to get experience. It's designed deliberately to mix people from different walks of life in a residential component for a couple of weeks, bridging social capital. Even then, we still had the concerns that the kids, as they walk in the door, are highly differentiated. Middle-class kids are self-confident. Often for kids from more disadvantaged backgrounds, they don't trust other people, with good reason sometimes. Can we do anything more about that? Well, we found that if you ran a 10-minute exercise at the beginning, where you ask people to talk about their similarities, it doesn't really change the levels of trust in the middle-class kids, but it makes a significant difference to the kids from more disadvantaged backgrounds. We know this stuff's really important, but we just didn't really know whether it's possible to move the dial on it. It's really bringing together some key academic literature, but then taking it further in quite a practical way.

HUMAN BEINGS ARE GROUP-ISH

One of the biggest problems is the thing that actually rips apart societies and economies is that human beings don't get on with each other. We see that across the world. There's something very flesh and blood about human beings, about how group-ish we are, and the way in which that's a part of our psychology. These are really interesting, deep questions about the nature of humans and about the forces in society pulling us apart or pushing us together, and they need a lot more working on before we can make much progress.

Valerie Curtis

on

THE SOURCES OF DISGUST

Think of cockroaches, other people's bodily fluids, a man sitting close to you on the bus whose face is covered in pustules, a toilet brush used to wash dishes. Yuck! Valerie Curtis has become a taxonomist of different types of disgust. She was professor at the London School of Hygiene and Tropical Medicine.

Listen to the podcast

https://www.socialsciencespace.com/2013/10/valerie-curtis-on-the-sources-of-disgust/

SOMETHING DISGUSTING IN A JAR

There have been lots of social scientists, psychologists, psychotherapists trying to puzzle out what the origins of disgust are, even cultural historians. There's a huge motley array of things that make us feel revolted, from filthy items, clothing, food, certain sorts of insects, even to moral disgust.

If I show you something disgusting in a jar, and you pull the lid off and have a sniff at it, you're going to feel a particular way. Your gut is going to churn, you're going to pull a distinctive face, which is like an 'Eugh' and is pretty much common throughout the globe. But more important than all of those things, you're actually going to stop and go 'I don't want to touch that thing, I don't want to look at it, I certainly don't want to eat it'. For me, it's that behavioural reaction that defines disgust.

DISGUST IS IN YOUR BRAIN

Disgust is a system in your brain that biases your behaviour to stop you coming into contact with things that might make you sick.

Studies have shown that if I tell you about somebody's disgusting behaviour, and somebody's morally disgusting behaviour, you'll pull the same face. You will report having similar feelings, and some of the same parts of your brain will light up.

There have been some social science experiments as well, which show that, if you think about having done something immoral, you are likely to want to wash your hands more. However, I think the evidence is still out on whether moral disgust and visceral disgust are the same thing.

IT GOES BACK TO INFECTIOUS DISEASE

If you line up all the things that people find disgusting, putting moral disgust aside, every single one of these things can be traced back to an infectious disease. I call this the Parasite Avoidance Theory of Disgust. In fact, your ancestor was probably quite squeamish and was actually quite good at avoiding things that might cause disease. So all of us are the descendants of people who had a good, strong sense of disgust.

We all, everywhere on the planet, share these basic themes of the things that we all find disgusting. There are no cultures where poo, for example, is something that people like. There are no cultures where sharing bodily fluids, except for a few exceptions, is something that is acceptable in any culture in the world. But there are differences.

We come equipped with a system that tells us to focus on certain things, and not on other things. We pay attention to the things that are biologically salient. I may see thousands of people walk past me, but the one that jumps out at me is the attractive man who might be a potential mate. I may see 24 plates of food go past me in a restaurant, but the one that smells bad, or looks funny is going to be the one that jumps out at me. If I taste it and it tastes bad, then I'm going to learn very quickly not to eat that sort of food again, and particularly not to go back to that restaurant again.

I think of disgust as a prototypical emotion, and I think we should be able to pull apart sub-domains to associate it with a particular task. Second, we use disgust in our work. Most of my work is actually in developing countries, trying to promote the avoidance of disease. Diarrhoeal diseases and respiratory infections kill more children than malaria, or HIV, or TB all put together, but they're much neglected, partly because they're disgusting conditions.

THE PROGRESSION FROM DISGUST TO MANNERS

Disgust is very much a double-edged sword. I'm hypothesising that there was a progression from disgust into manners. I have to learn a lot of good manners and rules that keep my bodily fluids away from you, otherwise you will be disgusted by me, and not want to interact with me. Also, I have to learn courtesy and rules that help me interact with you so that we can get all the benefits of social life.

The need to avoid pathogens was one of the first social tricks we had to learn in becoming the hyper-social beings that we are today. It's a big problem for society to solve. Some of our work on moral disgust shows also that we're deeply disgusted by lots of immoral behaviour, but particularly immoral behaviour that involves things like bodily fluids.

THE SOCIAL PARASITE

Also, there is the idea that if you're behaving like a social parasite, I'm going to be disgusted by you. There are many reasons for us to think that morality and disgust are linked.

MAKING SOCIAL CHANGE

Jennifer Richeson

on

PERCEPTIONS OF
RACIAL INEQUALITY

There is inequality in the United States, a fact most people accept and which data certainly bears out. But how bad do *you* think that inequality is, say, based on comparing the wealth held by the average Black person and the average white person in America? This is one of the questions that Jennifer Richeson, a social psychologist at Yale University, studies. She has news — bad news — about both the actual gap and what people think that gap is.

Listen to the podcast

https://www.socialsciencespace.com/2021/08/jennifer-richeson-on-perceptions-of-racial-inequality/

PERCEPTIONS OF THE BLACK-WHITE WEALTH GAP

Economists, both in government and outside, have done a great job measuring any number of disparities by social categories. In this case, we're talking about racial inequalities, in particular, racial economic inequality. The one that I focus on the most is the Black–white wealth gap, and it's staggeringly large. On average, as of 2016, the average Black family had about 10 per cent of the wealth of the average white family. So, if the average white family has $100, then the average Black family in America has about $10. This is huge. It's apparently gotten a little bit better, so maybe we're at about $12 or $13. But the important thing is it's a huge, staggering gap that has been persistent for 50/60 years.

We all are really surprised by how much disparity continues, especially in wealth, compared to what we believe. If you ask an average American, they will probably say that the wealth gap is around 65–70 per cent. It's a gap people acknowledge but it's much smaller than it actually is. It's very wrong compared to the actual wealth gap.

If you're motivated to believe that things are fair and just, when you're asked to provide these estimates, who comes to mind? There are economically successful African Americans such as Oprah, LeBron James, and other entertainers. We're trying to remind people that the richest Black Americans or the top Black billionaire is still number 76 on Forbes' list, and you can't even get their wealth on the same chart as Bezos or Zuckerberg. The magnitude is so incredibly different.

Part of the reason why we're so wrong is because we really believe that since the 1950s, '60s, '70s and '80s, things have gotten dramatically better, and are continuing to get better. So part of the reason people are so wrong today is because they think 'Well, yeah, there was a time when things were bad. Maybe in the '60s, maybe in the '70s, but we fixed all of that with laws and policies. And so now things are just fine, right?' Things are not fine. In fact, the racial wealth gap is almost as bad as it was in the '60s.

HIGHER INCOME AMERICANS ARE MORE INACCURATE

On average, higher income Americans are more inaccurate. And that's true across the sample. This is one interesting feature: higher income

Black Americans are less wrong compared to lower income Black Americans, than higher income white Americans are to lower income white Americans. Basically, in the United States, higher income Black Americans are still embedded in a more diverse network of friends, family, and community, both socially and economically, as well as racially, than higher income white Americans. Higher income white Americans by comparison are largely, both racially and socially, economically segregated in their lives, where they live, where they work, who they talk to. There is a clear distinction, a difference where upper middle class, Black Americans still have family members who are Black, and who are in probably less well-off circumstances, and they work with relatively high income white Americans. As a result of this, they get to see the contrast of how they live and how other people live, and that helps to inform accuracy on these matters.

STATUS THREAT

This is the idea that, as our nation is becoming more racially and ethnically and in some cases, religiously diverse, the groups that were dominant – meaning numerically, but also politically and economically dominant – are feeling some level of threat, concern and anxiety about what this new nation or set of people and these new circumstances that are way more diverse will mean for them. It's a vulnerability, and the sociology around this is usually called 'status threat'.

A concern about the standing of your group could be economic, it could be political, it could be cultural. Who gets to decide what holidays we celebrate and what monuments? We're contesting now in our country as to what types of people and heroes we honour publicly and whether we rethink their role in our society. All of that is being contested, in part because of the changing demographics of our nation. When you've had a bit of a monopoly on the say of how things run, then of course, any movement away from that and having these issues contested, is a bit threatening, or at least off-putting. The argument is that on average, as white Americans are thinking about this future, where their group is no longer more than 50 per cent of the population, that activates the status threat.

IS MERITOCRACY A LIE?

Meritocracy is fundamental to our individual wellbeing, but also our societal wellbeing, especially in the United States, which says that it is a meritocracy. However, you cannot be a meritocracy and have this kind of fundamental racial patterning of the goods of life, including longevity, at the same time. One has to be a lie. If it's the one that's our most sacred value, which is the American dream – pull yourself up, just work hard, you will achieve – if that is fundamentally wrong, and a lie, that is incompatible with who we understand ourselves to be, which is partly why people can't come to terms with the actual degree of racial inequality in society.

Perceptions of Racial Inequality

Jennifer Richeson

How bad do you think Inequality is?

For example, comparing the wealth of the average Black and White person in the U.S.A

Most guess it has greatly decreased over time, that equality is close

WRONG!

Wealth Inequality — Reality — Perception
1960 Time 2016

In 2016 the average Black family had ~10% of the wealth of the average White family

MASSIVE MISPERCEPTION

We feel compelled to conform to the narrative of racial progress

Changing Demographics & Status Threat

The Wealth GAP is Staggering and underpins other racial inequalities

TUNE IN!

Erica Chenoweth

on

NONVIOLENT RESISTANCE

Imagine you lived under a repressive dictatorship and wished to be part of a movement to overthrow it. What would be the best, the most effective tactics – terrorism, strikes, or demonstrations? Erica Chenoweth is a political scientist at Harvard, who researches political violence and alternatives to it, and has studied this question in depth. In 2014 Professor Chenoweth received the Karl Deutsch award, given annually by the International Studies Association to the scholar under 40 who has made the most significant impact on the field of international politics or peace research.

Listen to the podcast

https://www.socialsciencespace.com/2019/04/erica-chenoweth-on-nonviolent-resistance/

TECHNIQUES OF NONVIOLENT ACTION

There are hundreds, if not thousands, of different methods of nonviolent action. The technique involves any form of unarmed conflict where people actively confront an opponent without threatening or directly harming them physically. It can be a protest, a sit-in, a strike, a withdrawal of economic cooperation such as a boycott, or a withdrawal of social cooperation for example refusing to wear certain prescribed attire.

VIOLENT OR NONVIOLENT RESISTANCE: WHICH IS MORE SUCCESSFUL?

Nonviolent resistance on the whole is more successful than violent resistance. But nonviolent resistance in our data set historically was just as likely to fail as to succeed. It's just that there were twice as many successes than there were on the violent side. And of course, there are many known examples of successful violent uprisings, the Russian Revolution, the French Revolution, and the Algerian Revolution among them.

The Iranian Revolution, prior to turning into a violent consolidation of power under the Ayatollah, was primarily an unarmed mass campaign that overthrew the Shah. People estimate between five and 10 per cent of the population participated. They were also able to get oil workers from the countryside to defect to the opposition, as well as security forces.

Nonviolent resistance is easier to engage in, regardless of age, or physical ability. There are many different techniques of nonviolent action that are deliberately meant to be as inclusive as possible. That means more people can participate: women, children, elderly, people with disabilities, and people who are in ethnic minority groups who know they'll be surrounded by larger numbers of people. And that really reduces the chances that they themselves could be hurt.

The second reason it's so inclusive is that it's easier to improvise participation, meaning that you don't have to give up your day job and go underground if you're going to just be another kind of faceless member of a crowd. And the third reason is, it's usually easier to figure out how to participate, meaning if you're wanting to join an armed group, most armed groups recruit members through knowing someone and through channels that are social in nature, whereas with mass movements, you know where to go if you want to participate.

NONVIOLENT CAMPAIGNS LEADING TO DEMOCRATIC TRANSITION

We do find evidence that nonviolent campaigns are much likelier to be followed by a democratic transition than violent campaigns because violence is deeply polarising. It further segments the population into those who control the means of military power, and those who are the victims of it. It's almost impossible to conjure up cases where there was a successful, violent revolution that was followed by a democratic transition, at least in the short term.

THE DIGITAL REVOLUTION IS A DOUBLE-EDGED SWORD

The digital revolution has been a double-edged sword for these movements. Digital technology makes it easier to organise protests, but I don't think that necessarily means it's easier to organise campaigns. So you can get large numbers of people to the streets in very short order, but to keep people engaged and participating, and to come up with strategies that will lead to the defection of security forces and economic businesses, requires a much longer term, well planned strategy. The downside for the digital revolution therefore is that it might give people a false sense that all they have to do is turnout hundreds of thousands of people in the streets without doing the significant planning and preparation required to sustain that level of participation.

For example, some people argue that in the early cases of the Arab Spring, Tunisia and Egypt, there had been years of organising before those end games came to pass. But people observing from other nearby countries thought, well, all we have to do is pour into the streets. And they were watching the end game, not the decades of groundwork that led to the ousters of Ben Ali and Mubarak.

Alison Liebling
on
SUCCESSFUL PRISONS

ABOUT THIS PODCAST

In determining what makes a successful prison,
where would you place 'trust'? Alison Liebling,
a criminologist at the University of Cambridge
and the director of the Institute of Criminology's
Prisons Research Centre, says its role is neglected.
As she tells interviewer David Edmonds, she
believes what makes a prison good is the existence
and the practice of intelligent trust.

Listen to
the podcast

USING APPRECIATIVE INQUIRY

Appreciative Inquiry is not a research tool, or at least it wasn't until I adapted it. It's a term that is used in organisation or economic development. This methodology assumes that if you put people and organisations in touch with what gives them life and energy, then they will grow in that direction. It reverses the typical social science preoccupation with problems and instead of 'Tell me about your offending again', you ask 'Tell me about something you're most proud of in your life'.

THE HUMAN SIDE OF PRISON LIFE

People are more at risk out on the streets than they are in a prison, and not all prisoners are dangerous. A prison setting is probably one of the most controlled and supervised environments you can imagine. The first research project I ever did was in 1986 and it was in a young offender institution. I didn't know what to expect, but I was interviewing young offenders about whether what they did in prison was linked to what they did outside. On day one, I realised all my assumptions were wrong. The prisoners there were young and they were frightened. Some of them cried. A lot of them reminded me of people I knew, they were very ordinary, a bit scared. A lot of them had difficulty speaking in the interview, because they didn't expect to be listened to. I had to do quite a lot of work reassuring them that it was okay to talk, that they could be heard; they were actually very vulnerable. The last thing you think about when you walk into a prison is danger. The human side of prison life is so dominant. People look after you. They make jokes, they offer you tea, they're curious about you. They're human institutions.

PRISON OFFICERS AS READERS OF HUMAN BEHAVIOUR

One of the things that prison officers do that people don't appreciate, is they are very subtle readers of human behaviour. They learn a lot of that in the job, it's in their skin and bones. By the time they've been doing the job for a few years, they read situations really well. What they're doing is making judgements about gradations of trust. Can I let this prisoner out? Can I trust this prisoner to do something for another prisoner?

Should I give this prisoner a job on the wing? They're continually making these kinds of judgements, and they have to know their prisoners really well. If that stops, the whole prison stops.

One of the frustrations that prisoners express, especially when they get caught up in long sentences, is that they want to be downgraded in security categories and they will want to apply for parole. How do they demonstrate trustworthiness? They're always looking for opportunities to demonstrate trustworthiness, and they find it gets ignored or over-looked or it doesn't get written down.

A turning point for the prison service occurred around 1987, 1988. It had been in quite a bad place. Lots of things were done around that time, including some changes in the way prisons were thought about and managed. Also, in 1990 there were watershed disturbances, such as the Strangeways disturbance, and 30 other riots. There was a major inquiry by Lord Justice Woolf and there were significant developments and improvements; suicide rates were reduced, and violence was reduced; there was a decency agenda. So, there was major improvement. More recently, I think the agenda that's taken over is more imprisonment for less money and I think we've gone too far in that direction.

BEING IN DIALOGUE

It's a privilege to be an academic who is in conversation with people who run prisons and think about prison policy. In that sense, the fact that there is a dialogue improves our work because they ask tough questions and they only listen to real evidence; it keeps us on our toes. But there's the downside. The world of policy has just got faster and faster. It's got further and further away from evidence. They are so constrained themselves, that they're not asking the question we want to be asked, which is, how do we make all prisons as good as this prison? This relationship can be a very constrained one, and they want answers tomorrow. We want three years to do the job properly. Our worlds are a little bit in conflict and tension, but it's better that we're in dialogue than not.

Lawrence Sherman

on

EXPERIMENTAL CRIMINOLOGY

There are many theories about crime, its causes and treatment. So how do we decide which ones are effective? Take the case of restorative justice when criminals and their victims meet face to face. Some critics argue that this approach is too soft on perpetrators and doesn't work. But is this true? Lawrence Sherman, a professor at Cambridge University, believes that theories about crime can and should be put to the test. He's a passionate advocate of experimental criminology.

Listen to the podcast

DEFINED BY A METHOD

Experimental criminology is a field that is defined by a method, much like experimental physics or experimental biology. The method of course embraces a wide range of questions, but in the case of criminology, it's a bit more profound in its implications. For most of its history, criminology has been essentially a descriptive or observational science, sort of like astronomy.

By developing a field of experimental criminology, what we accept is that the core concerns of a discipline of criminology have to be how societies make decisions – and what decisions they should make – to deal with their crime problems. That goes well beyond the descriptive and the observational, the purely theoretical. It requires having very hard empirical evidence, especially randomised control trials, which is the primary method in experimental criminology.

SOCIAL SCIENCE AS A SOURCE OF SOCIAL CRITIQUE

Most criminologists alive today would have been heavily influenced by the role of social science in the latter twentieth century as a source of social criticism, as a source of values that were contrary to convention-al values at the time: greater tolerance for diverse lifestyles, greater human rights – lots of good things that social science was associated with.

THE MILWAUKEE EXPERIMENT

An experiment was done in Milwaukee from 1987 to 1988, one that we have followed up for 24 years. Milwaukee was the experiment in which we first found that the effect of arrest depended on whether the suspect was employed. Among the unemployed suspects, arrest doubled the rate of repeat domestic violence and cut it in half among employed suspects. So the question was, how long would that last? Many other things happened in their lives, such as getting arrested for other crimes, changing economic conditions. Most theorists, I think, would say that the impact of a randomly assigned arrest in 1987 or '88 is unlikely to persist into 2012, and they would be wrong.

In fact, the effects got bigger around 12 and 15 years out, and the negative effect of arrest on unemployed people is the most powerful persisting effect. There's no positive benefit from arresting employed people that lasted 24 years. There was a slight difference, but it wasn't what we call statistically significant: it could've been due to chance. But what was clearly not due to chance was the 24-year impact of causing more domestic violence among people who were arrested and unemployed.

DESIGNING A TEST FOR RESTORATIVE JUSTICE

In the mid-1990s, the Australian National University asked me to help design a test of a very old method of dealing with crime that they call restorative justice. The experiment was in Canberra, and police identified people who they thought might be appropriate for a meeting between victim and offender with the victim's family and the offender's family. Instead of prosecuting them in court they would be diverted to this meeting, led by a police officer and at the end of the meeting there would be an agreement that the offender would do something to try to repair the harm to the victim.

The success was holding a conference and then having everybody walk out of the conference saying 'Yes, this was a good thing to do'. And according to the victims, they felt much better having gone to the conference and they certainly felt much less angry than victims who didn't have a chance to have this kind of conference and apology. The offenders actually felt terribly ashamed and there's some evidence they were traumatised by it. They were actually reliving the conference in future days, months, years ahead, having nightmares about it, racing thoughts about how angry some of the people were in the room.

THE END APPEARS TO BE LESS REPEAT OFFENDING

It's a means to an end, and the end appears to be less repeat offending. The best you can get by way of reducing repeat offending is something we achieved without ever taking these people to court. It is also much cheaper and much quicker with far higher levels of victim satisfaction.

It's an option that's much more potentially damaging psychologically than just sitting in your prison cell and having your lawyer do all your talking for you. Damaging psychologically in the sense that it is painful in the moment, not necessarily damaging in the long run. We have had people who've led miserable lives, one of whom has written a book about his experience in restorative justice. This experience for him got him out of a career of 5,000 burglaries. As far as he's concerned, even though he still remembers the trauma of that conference, it's the best thing that ever happened to him in his life.

EXPLAINING THE PRESENT AND THE UNEXPECTED

Hetan Shah

on

SOCIAL SCIENCE AND THE PANDEMIC

ABOUT THIS PODCAST

This podcast was recorded in April 2020 – only a few months into the Covid-19 pandemic. The pandemic has and will continue to mutate the social landscape of the world, but amid the lost lives and spoiled economies, in its wake has come a new appreciation of what science and scientists contribute. 'You don't have to go back many months,' says Hetan Shah, the chief executive of the British Academy, 'for a period when politicians were relatively dismissive of experts – and then suddenly we've seen a shift now to where they've moved very close to scientists. And generally that's a very good thing.'

Listen to the podcast

https://www.socialsciencespace.com/2020/04/hetan-shah-on-social-science-and-the-pandemic/

NOT JUST A MEDICAL PHENOMENON

Governments have recognised that the Covid-19 pandemic is not just a medical phenomenon, but a social and economic one. If you look at the thinking that's gone on around how best to get people to wash their hands, there was behavioural science in which advert was most effective, or the whole thing about singing happy birthday twice, which was a way of remembering how long we should spend washing our hands. On a completely different level, you couldn't have predicted from the Conservative manifesto that they would end up with a furlough scheme, putting millions of workers on the government payroll to keep their jobs alive. Economists have clearly been involved in all of that.

HELPING US THINK ABOUT THE IMPORTANCE OF SOCIAL NORMS

Behavioural psychology has been very helpful in helping us think about the importance of social norms. For example, when the press early on was saying, 'Lots of people are breaking the rules and going out to the park'. Behavioural psychology shows that's not a good thing to be doing; it's much better to be promoting the fact that most people are staying indoors, and that promotion is more likely to lead to people following the rules. If you promote the few people that are breaking the rules, that's more likely to instigate others to break the rules.

A different example which was in the news was the issue around ethnic minorities who seem to be more vulnerable to the disease, and the medical sciences' focus on some of the genetic components around why that might be the case. But sociologists might be looking at the social components. Part of that might be, for example, are people from ethnic minorities typically less well off? There might also be things around the job roles that they have, or that they're more likely to work in the NHS, or in doing deliveries or in shops, which might then lead to diseases spreading. The other favourite of mine is anthropologists who wouldn't have been at all surprised by the panic buying of toilet paper, because of the cultural and symbolic importance of things like cleanliness and security in times of crisis.

One of the things that the psychology and behavioural sciences show is that we all suffer from a range of biases. And of course, the key insight is that our leaders suffer them too. We all suffer from a kind of optimism bias, a kind of exponential myopia. These are the kinds of things that social science can help us see. I think it can make us look with more kindness upon our leaders, because we realise that they are human too.

LEARNING FROM WELLBEING DATA

The interesting things we can track are the data on how the pandemic itself has affected us. There'll be so many interesting things to learn from wellbeing data: how did people fare and feel in the lockdown? We have found in the past that people's wellbeing can be difficult to predict. It may well be that for certain groups, their wellbeing has adjusted, and they found ways to cope, which would be great, but we don't yet know. And similarly, measuring their consumption data: what did we eat and drink? There's bigger and deeper things, such as poverty and unemployment, which are likely to be going up, and we will see those results impact on mental health.

There's so many other changes that we're seeing in working patterns. Will any of these stick? Are we going to see more remote working and more virtual meetings? There'll be all sorts of fascinating data about how the pandemic has affected us. One twist in all of this, of course, is that the pandemic is also affecting the research community itself, and the future of higher education, which is really going to be taking a hit. One worry is that there may be fewer social scientists who are around or who have the funding to actually look at some of this data.

CAN WE REIMAGINE OUR WAY TO A MORE SUSTAINABLE AND FAIR SOCIETY?

Social psychology suggests behaviour change requires unfreezing existing behaviour patterns before new patterns can be created. The reason that's so difficult is so many of our behaviours are based on social norms. It's very hard to do behaviour change at an individual level. The task for social scientists is not just to understand and explain but also for social imagination. Can we reimagine our way to a more sustainable and fair society, thinking about how we can improve wellbeing for all we've noticed from this, that there are many people that we rely on but the economy doesn't always value? People working in care, nurses, bus drivers: can we build an economy that values them more? This all sounds a bit utopian, and perhaps it won't go anywhere. But it does seem to me to be a really important role for social scientists and I think it's worth a shot.

AFTERWORD

The British Academy, where Hetan Shah is chief executive, in March 2021 published *The Covid Decade*, a major report on the long-term societal impacts of the pandemic, drawing together a wide range of social science material.

You may think that you are immune to supernatural attitudes or beliefs: they're for others, for more primitive, more superstitious types. But Bruce Hood, Professor of Developmental Psychology in Society at Bristol University, says supernatural beliefs are much more common than you think. Rather than collect ectoplasm, Hood focuses on why human beings, starting as children, offer supernatural explanations for natural occurrences.

Listen to
the podcast

ESSENTIALISM AND ATTRIBUTING A HIDDEN DIMENSION TO THINGS

When I was a young boy I'd watch Uri Geller doing these amazing things and I really did believe there must be something to this because everyone was saying he has all these abilities. I wanted to do psychology to learn how to use my mind to control the physical world and all that sort of nonsense.

My particular research interest is a field known as essentialism. This is the attribution of a hidden dimension to things giving them their true identity. It's almost as if there's a sort of spiritual component. When you start to think about essentialism you can see it operating every-where, not only in supernatural thinking, but also in the way that we think about what makes things irreplaceable. I'm fascinated by this sort of crossover between natural reasoning and then this sort of emergence of supernatural assumptions.

The example I usually give is a wedding ring. I say to people, 'This is your wedding ring, would you be happy to swap it for an identical wed-ding ring?' And most people, if they're enjoying a happy marriage, will say 'No.' Then you say, 'Why not?' and they say, 'Well because it's not the original.' But the trouble with things being original is that there are some metaphysical issues about what constitutes an original item.

WE HOLD DEEP-SEATED BELIEFS ABOUT TRUE IDENTITY

When we form emotional attachments to significant others, then we essentialise them. We think there's a property which makes them irre-placeable. We hold deep-seated beliefs about retaining true authentic-ity and true identity. It is the same with works of art. As soon as you discover it's not by who you thought it was it loses some of its, not only financial value, but emotional attachment.

We're now actually doing work where we get people to put on or touch clothing and then we inform them that it belongs to someone very good or someone very evil and then we watch what happens afterwards. Do they wash their hands? Do they start doing all these implicit measures? And they all suggest that they are acting irrationally. But there's a good reason why they might do so. We don't know why people are crazed kill-ers. There might be a biological contamination. So in that sense, it's not an entirely irrational response. But when you explain it explicitly, people say, 'Well I know it's a bit strange, but it just makes me feel yucky.'

SUPERNATURAL THINKING

That's what I mean by supernatural thinking, because if these things were really real, if these dimensions and forces and energies were real, they wouldn't be supernatural, they'd be natural. These are things which go beyond our current understanding.

Religion is just organised supernatural thinking. Every religion has to have entities who have supernatural powers. I think part of that works because of the pool of the supernatural. There's something which transcends the mundane and so it has to have supernatural qualities. But religions are just organised structures. They're narratives about the beginnings of the universe, the ends of the universe, why we're on this planet, and where we go when we're dead. Whereas people can be non-religious and yet still believe in a whole variety of supernatural things. I think the difference is only one is organised supernatural thinking, the other is just spontaneous belief systems.

IS IT ALL LEARNED, OR IS IT INDOCTRINATION?

If you're Richard Dawkins then you'll argue it's indoctrination. Or is there a natural inclination? I think as with many things in psychology, it's a combination of the two. There are predispositions that actually explain why one brother will become very religious and the other one might become an ardent atheist. There's always variation. And the studies which have looked for the shared likelihood of these, for example twin studies, do support the idea that there's some genetic basis for it. My suggestion is that we're trip-wired to seeing structured order and inferring causes and then whether or not they become full blown supernatural religious ideas really depends on the culture in which you're raised.

A lot of magical things, superstitious behaviours or rituals, are to do with controlling uncontrollable events. This is why you see them at major transitions in life: birth, death, financial, marriages, all the major ceremonies which mark the important times in our lives have rituals associated with them. And these rituals are to try and control events which are not necessarily controllable.

SOCIAL SCIENCE BITES PRESENTS...

THE SUPERNATURAL
BRUCE HOOD

You probably have Supernatural beliefs

9 out of 10 think they know if they are being watched

The brain is a sophisticated pattern recognition machine

It tries to causally connect events

Seeking Control
Birth → Fate
Luck → Death
over the uncontrollable

ESSENTIALISM
Attributing hidden forces to things

Sentimental Value Objects

Magical Qualities ♂ wedding rings

why does damaging a portrait feel so wrong?

Religion as Organised Supernatural Thinking

The Ship of Theseus and the Metaphysics of "Originals"

TUNE IN!